EDGE BOOKS

Epic Disasters

# THE WORST AVALANCHES OF ALL TIME

by Suzanne Garbe

Consultant:
Susan L. Cutter, PhD
Director
Hazards and Vulnerability Research Institute
University of South Carolina

CAPSTONE PRESS
a capstone imprint

Edge Books are published by Capstone Press,
1710 Roe Crest Drive, North Mankato, Minnesota 56003.
www.capstonepub.com

*Library of Congress Cataloging-in-Publication Data*
Garbe, Suzanne.
 The worst avalanches of all time / by Suzanne Garbe.
  p. cm. — (Edge books. Epic disasters)
 Summary: "Describes the worst avalanches in history, as well as causes, types, and
disaster tips"— Provided by publisher.
 Includes index.
 ISBN 978-1-4296-8417-0 (library binding)
 ISBN 978-1-62065-219-0 (ebook PDF)
 1. Avalanches—Juvenile literature.  I. Title.
 QC929.A8G37 2013
 363.34'9—dc23                          2012002611

**Editorial Credits**
Kristen Mohn, editor; Gene Bentdahl and Kazuko Collins, designers;
    Marcie Spence, media researcher; Laura Manthe, production specialist

**Photo Credits**
Alamy: Ashley Cooper, 29, Interfoto, 11; AP Images: John Heliprin, 21
(top), Musadeq Sadeq, 24, Stacy Standley, 21 (bottom); Avalanche in the
full-scale avalanche dynamics test site of the WSL Institute for Snow and
Avalanche Research SLF, Davos, cover, 1; Bridgeman Art Library: Look
and Learn, 7; Corbis: 12, Amit Gupta/Reuters, 15, Anatoly Maltsev/
epa, 9, Bettmann, 16, Julien Hekimian/Sygma, 18; Getty Images:
Hulton Archive, 22; iStockphoto: RafalBelzowski, 5; Shutterstock:
Wansfordphoto, 26-27

Printed in the United States of America in Stevens Point, Wisconsin.
032012    006678WZF12

# TABLE of CONTENTS

# A WALL OF SNOW

Avalanches happen suddenly and without warning. People nearby might hear rumbling as loud as a thousand trains. They might feel the ground shake. Before they know it, a wall of snow is moving toward them. It charges at more than 200 miles (322 kilometers) per hour. Everything in its path is destroyed.

An avalanche is a large amount of **debris** that plunges down a mountainside. It might include rocks, soil, and mud. However, the word more commonly refers to slides of snow and ice.

Three things are necessary for an avalanche to happen:

- a slope with an angle of 30 to 40 degrees
- unstable **snowpack**
- a trigger or cause

A natural cause might be a snowstorm or heavy rain. A rise in temperature, an earthquake, or a volcanic eruption are other possible natural causes. But the trigger could also be human activity, such as an explosion. It might even be something as small as the weight of a single person skiing down a mountain.

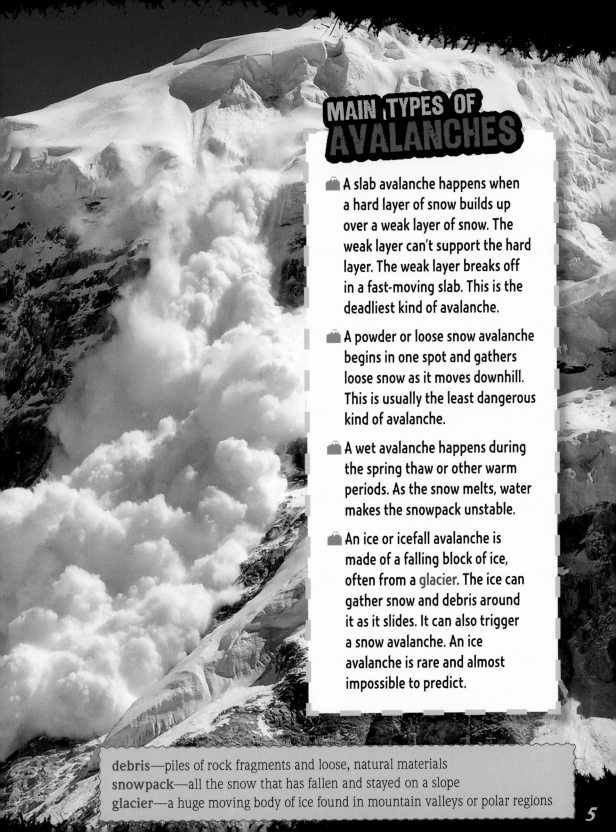

# MAIN TYPES OF AVALANCHES

- A slab avalanche happens when a hard layer of snow builds up over a weak layer of snow. The weak layer can't support the hard layer. The weak layer breaks off in a fast-moving slab. This is the deadliest kind of avalanche.

- A powder or loose snow avalanche begins in one spot and gathers loose snow as it moves downhill. This is usually the least dangerous kind of avalanche.

- A wet avalanche happens during the spring thaw or other warm periods. As the snow melts, water makes the snowpack unstable.

- An ice or icefall avalanche is made of a falling block of ice, often from a glacier. The ice can gather snow and debris around it as it slides. It can also trigger a snow avalanche. An ice avalanche is rare and almost impossible to predict.

debris—piles of rock fragments and loose, natural materials
snowpack—all the snow that has fallen and stayed on a slope
glacier—a huge moving body of ice found in mountain valleys or polar regions

# ANCIENT AVALANCHE

DATE: early October 218 BC
LOCATION: the Alps, Italy

Hannibal was one of the greatest military generals of all time. More than 2,000 years ago, he led the army of Carthage, an ancient city in North Africa. Carthage wanted to invade its enemy, Rome. So Hannibal's army and many animals trekked across the Italian Alps. When they reached the peak of the mountains, they camped for two days. Fresh snow covered their path, hiding an older crust of snow. As the troops headed down the mountain toward Rome, the animals' feet broke through the top layer, triggering several avalanches. Soldiers and animals were swept down the mountain. In the end, 18,000 men, 2,000 horses, and several elephants lost their lives.

# THE COLLAPSED GLACIER

DATE: September 20, 2002
LOCATION: Caucasus Mountains, Russia

The Caucasus Mountains in Russia are topped year-round with snow and ice. Tourists and hikers love visiting the region. In September 2002 one of Russia's most popular actors, Sergei Bodrov Jr., was filming a movie there. High above the film crew was a mass of ice called the Kolka Glacier. Without warning, it broke away from the 15,700-foot (4,785-meter) peak of the mountain. Scientists aren't sure what caused the glacier to break. It dashed 8 miles (13 km) down the slope, bringing ice, snow, and debris with it. Moving at more than 100 miles (161 km) per hour, it destroyed several villages. The avalanche also killed Bodrov and more than 120 other people.

The collapse of the Kolka Glacier is the largest collapse of a glacier ever recorded. It carried a huge amount of material. In one spot ice from the avalanche was piled 39 stories high. It took years for all the ice to melt. Today scientists continue to study the area to learn more about the massive avalanche.

# WAR IN THE ALPS

**DATE:** various dates, 1915–1918
**LOCATION:** Tyrolean Alps between Italy and Austria

During World War I (1914–1918), Austrian and Italian troops fought in the mountains between their two countries. Many avalanches occurred naturally during these years and killed unprepared soldiers. However, soldiers also discovered they could purposely cause avalanches. They did this by firing explosives at the snow above their enemies. On a single day, 235 men died in the village of Marmolada. However, it was not just this deadly day that made history. It was the months and years of avalanches that battered these troops. The death toll in these battles was far greater than that of similar battles fought on flat ground. The loss of life between 1915 and 1918 was between 40,000 and 80,000 soldiers.

War isn't the only time people cause avalanches on purpose. Sometimes explosives are used to start avalanches when a snowpack seems unstable. The state of Washington briefly closes roads to trigger avalanches that might otherwise threaten passing cars.

Austrian soldiers march through an Italian glacier.

# TRAGEDY ON THE TRACKS

**DATE:** March 1, 1910
**LOCATION:** Wellington, Washington

Passengers on the Great Northern Railway local train Number 25 were finishing a bad week. Their train had already experienced several problems on the trip across Washington. Small avalanches had slowed it down twice. By Friday the train was stranded after heavy snow blocked its path. A second train carrying mail arrived and was forced to stop as well. Most of the passengers stayed aboard while workers spent two days trying to clear the snow.

On Monday they were still stranded when a blizzard became a rainstorm complete with thunder and lightning. The rain made the top layer of snow soft. On early Tuesday morning, an enormous slab avalanche broke away from the snowpack above the train. The slab was 1.5 miles (2.4 km) long and 0.25 mile (0.4 km) wide. It crashed down the mountain and swept both trains over a cliff and into a ravine.

Rescue workers were able to save 23 people. Ninety-six other passengers and crew members died in the avalanche. The snow and wreckage took three weeks to clean up. It remains the worst snow disaster in U.S. history.

FACT:
In the western half of the United States alone, there are an estimated 100,000 avalanches every year.

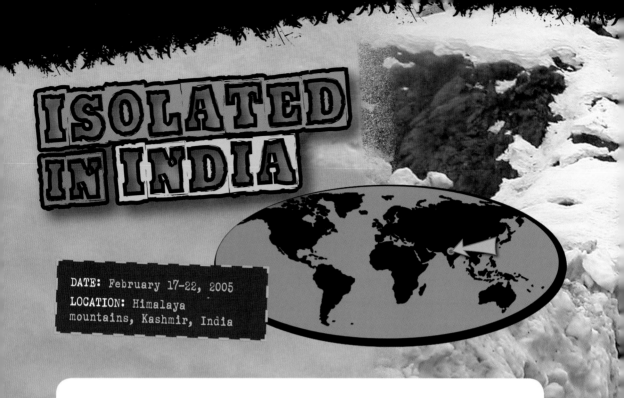

# ISOLATED IN INDIA

DATE: February 17-22, 2005
LOCATION: Himalaya
mountains, Kashmir, India

Over the course of six days in February 2005, as much as 16 feet (4.9 m) of fresh snow fell in Kashmir, India. The Indian government knew the risk of an avalanche was high. Even so, they weren't able to protect all their citizens from the disaster to come.

Countless massive avalanches affected a broad area throughout Kashmir. Electricity was cut off. Temperatures dropped to minus 29 degrees Fahrenheit (minus 34 degrees Celsius). Thousands of people were stranded on a highway for nearly a week after snow blocked the roads. Homes were buried under as much as 18 feet (5.5 m) of snow. In some distant villages, the government dropped food and blankets from military helicopters to help survivors.

Traffic begins moving again on a highway that was closed for 12 days after the 2005 avalanche.

It took weeks to reach all the areas hit by the avalanches. Even then rescue workers weren't sure how many people had died. The villages were too spread out and difficult to reach. The Indian government estimates that more than 400 people died in the avalanches. Another 2 million people were affected by the storms that triggered the slides.

# A MATTER OF MINUTES

Rescuers search for victims in the snow and mud after the 1962 avalanche.

One of the deadliest avalanches in history was caused by a broken glacier. In less than 10 minutes, thousands of people died.

The glacier was perched at the top of 21,834-foot- (6,655-m-) high Mount Huascarán in Peru. Heavy snowfall and warming temperatures in January 1962 made the glacier unstable. A piece of the glacier cracked off. Three million tons (2.7 million metric tons) of ice came crashing down the mountain. Along the way it swept up dirt, boulders, sheep, and even houses. It flattened four villages and killed 800 people.

Then a series of hills made the avalanche change course. The town of Ranrahirca lay in the avalanche's new path. It killed almost everyone there—a staggering 2,700 people. The avalanche killed a total of about 3,500 people.

FACT:
A second deadly avalanche occurred on Mount Huascarán eight years later in 1970. This avalanche was triggered by a massive earthquake and killed about 18,000 people.

# FAILURE IN THE ALPS

DATE: February 9, 1999
LOCATION: Montroc, France

## FACT:

Over the last 50 years, the French Alps have become a popular place for winter sports. As a result, towns are growing and many buildings are being constructed in avalanche-prone areas.

In January 1999, Montroc was a small resort village in the French Alps. The snow had started early that year, and people were enjoying the perfect winter weather.

However, a period of dry weather followed. It caused a thin layer of ice to form on the snow. Then, in early February, more than 6.5 feet (2 m) of snow fell over a three-day period. The old layer of thin ice made a weak base for the heavy new snow. The high winds that arrived with the snow were another danger. Conditions were ripe for an avalanche.

Montroc was governed by the nearby town of Chamonix. Officials there considered telling Montroc's villagers to **evacuate**. But they waited too long. As they met on February 9, the region's biggest avalanche in 40 years descended on Montroc. A massive slab of snow slammed down the mountain at 60 miles (97 km) per hour. It killed 12 people and destroyed 14 buildings. The remains of the village were buried under 100,000 tons (91,000 metric tons) of snow.

Many people were angry that the mayor of Chamonix had not evacuated the village. They believed he should have acted sooner to save lives. The mayor was brought to trial and convicted of second-degree murder.

avalanche-prone—likely for an avalanche to occur
evacuate—to leave an area during a time of danger

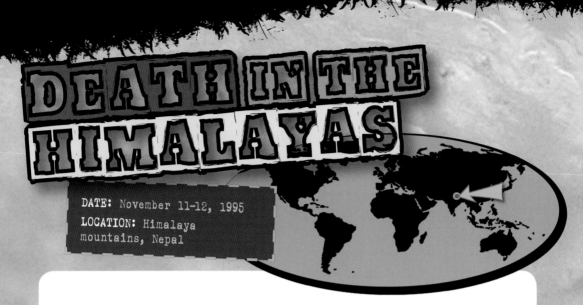

# DEATH IN THE HIMALAYAS

**DATE:** November 11-12, 1995
**LOCATION:** Himalaya mountains, Nepal

Mount Everest in the Himalaya mountains is the world's tallest mountain. Each year 65,000 climbers and hikers travel to Nepal to visit the Himalayas. Most don't climb the tall peaks but hike across valleys and view Mount Everest from below. That view is what brought 13 Japanese hikers to the area in 1995.

On the night before the avalanche, the group went to sleep in a camp alongside 11 local guides. Perhaps no one in the group knew about the 6 feet (1.8 m) of new snow that had fallen in the region during the past week. Or maybe they simply didn't realize how dangerous the fresh snow might be. At 1:00 a.m. a new snowstorm triggered an avalanche. Snow barreled toward the camp while everyone slept. All 13 Japanese visitors died, as well as the 11 guides and two local citizens. Takashi Miyahara traveled by helicopter to the site with rescuers the next day. He said, "We could only see rooftops of the huts where the trekkers were staying." Officials believe it to be the worst avalanche disaster ever to strike a hiking **expedition** in Nepal.

shelter where the Japanese hikers were buried

tourists hiking in the Himalayas

expedition—a journey with a goal, such as exploring or searching for something

# THE WINTER OF TERROR

**DATE:** various dates,
winter 1950-1951

**LOCATION:** the Alps,
Austria and Switzerland

In the winter of 1950–1951 Austria and Switzerland were experiencing some of the heaviest snowfalls the countries had ever seen. That winter more than 265 people were killed by a series of avalanches throughout the region. It came to be known as "the winter of terror."

A single day—January 20, 1951—was responsible for most of the season's deaths. The conditions were perfect for an avalanche. A mix of heavy snow and rain had caused the snowpack to be very unstable. As a result, not just one but several avalanches pounded the Alps that day.

Trees had been planted to help slow avalanches in the area. However, the rush of falling snow caused hurricane-strength winds to head down the mountain before it. The wind knocked over the trees, clearing the way for the avalanches to rocket down the mountain. Dozens of towns and famous ski resorts were destroyed. The Swiss village of Vals was wiped away entirely. Roads and railways were blocked. By the end of the day, 240 people were dead.

**FACT:**

Many governments in avalanche-prone areas take steps to protect people and buildings. These steps include using stronger construction materials and planting trees to slow or redirect avalanches. Wind baffles can also keep snow from drifting to particular areas.

baffle—a human-made object designed to stop or change the movement of something

# THE HIGH MOUNTAIN ROAD

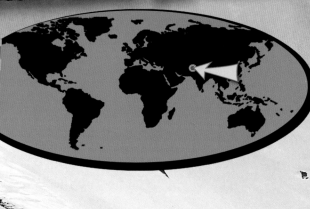

**DATE:** February 8-9, 2010
**LOCATION:** Salang Pass, Afghanistan

The Salang Pass is a high mountain road in Afghanistan. It connects the capital city, Kabul, to the city Mazar-i-Sharif in the north. At 11,000 feet (3,353 m) tall, the Salang Pass is nearly ten times as high as the Empire State Building. It is one of the highest roads in the world. The pass is traveled daily by 16,000 vehicles.

**Meteorologists** can predict heavy snowfall. But avalanches can rarely be predicted. When more than 24 avalanches hit the Salang Pass region in just three days in early February 2010, no one was warned. Strong winds and heavy rain caused the avalanches. The avalanches trapped hundreds of people in a tunnel and pushed other vehicles off the road into a **gorge**. Dozens of people were injured, and 175 people died.

After the disaster the American military helped Afghan teams deal with the crisis. Together they evacuated thousands of people and brought aid to the injured survivors.

meteorologist—a person who studies and predicts the weather
gorge—a canyon with steep walls that rise straight upward

FACT:
In many places avalanches occur again and again. Avalanches have hit the Salang Pass countless times, including in 1993, 1997, 1998, and 2002. Each of these avalanches took the lives of as many as 100 people.

# THE SUMMER AVALANCHE

DATE: July 12, 1892
LOCATION: St. Gervais,
Switzerland

Mont Blanc is the highest peak in the Alps. It's also where one of Switzerland's deadliest avalanches occurred. The mountain looms over two Swiss resort towns. Although the Alps are known for their avalanches, nobody expected one there in the summer. Tourists were enjoying the area's natural hot springs and grand hotels. Snow and avalanches were probably far from anyone's mind.

Then on the night of July 12, 1892, a massive glacier broke off the side of Mont Blanc. It swept down the mountain, carrying snow, rocks, trees, and debris toward the towns below. It happened too quickly for anyone to be warned. Nearly every building in the two towns was destroyed. The death toll was 140 people. Only 10 residents of the two towns survived.

FACT:

Switzerland has more avalanche deaths than any other country in the world.

St. Gervais, Switzerland

# LIVING WITH AVALANCHES

If you're visiting any snowy slope of 30 to 40 degrees, you need to be prepared for the possibility of an avalanche. Consider taking an avalanche safety course. Or take a trained guide with you. He or she can dig holes in the snow to see if the snowpack is stable. Additionally, a few key supplies can help you deal with an avalanche emergency:

- An avalanche **beacon** produces a radio signal that will help rescuers find you if you're buried in snow.
- An avalanche probe is a long pole you push through snow piles to locate a buried person.
- A shovel will help you dig through snow and debris to reach a buried person.

beacon—a small radio transmitter that can be worn; beacons help rescue workers find victims lost in an avalanche

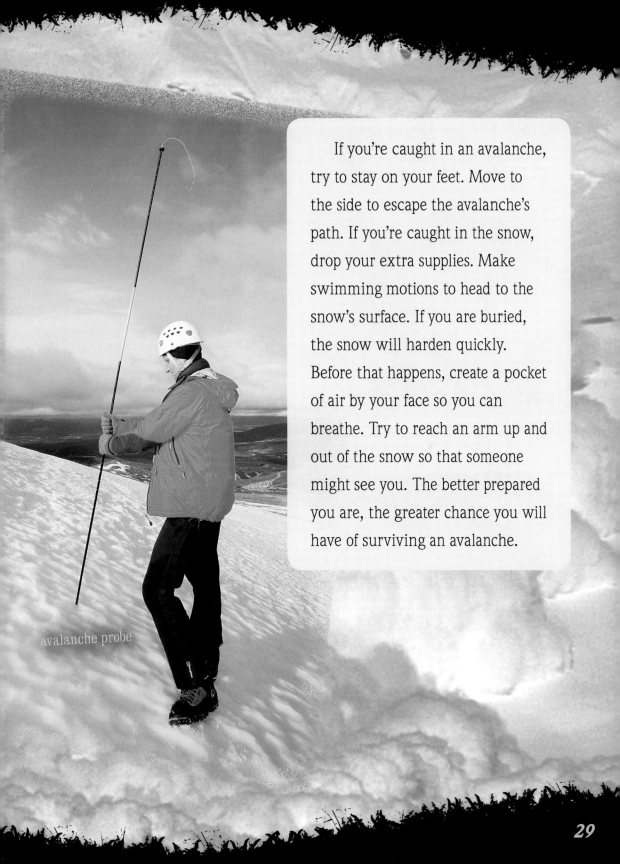

If you're caught in an avalanche, try to stay on your feet. Move to the side to escape the avalanche's path. If you're caught in the snow, drop your extra supplies. Make swimming motions to head to the snow's surface. If you are buried, the snow will harden quickly. Before that happens, create a pocket of air by your face so you can breathe. Try to reach an arm up and out of the snow so that someone might see you. The better prepared you are, the greater chance you will have of surviving an avalanche.

avalanche probe

# GLOSSARY

**avalanche-prone** (AV-uh-lanch PROHN)—likely for an avalanche to occur

**baffle** (BAF-uhl)—a human-made object designed to stop or change the movement of something

**beacon** (BEE-kuhn)—a small radio transmitter that can be worn; beacons help rescue workers find victims lost in an avalanche

**debris** (duh-BREE)—piles of rock fragments and loose, natural materials

**evacuate** (i-VA-kyuh-wayt)—to leave an area during a time of danger

**expedition** (ek-spuh-DIH-shuhn)—a journey with a goal, such as exploring or searching for something

**glacier** (GLAY-shur)—a huge moving body of ice found in mountain valleys or polar regions

**gorge** (GORJ)—a canyon with steep walls that rise straight upward

**meteorologist** (mee-tee-ur-AWL-uh-jist)—a person who studies and predicts the weather

**snowpack** (SNOH-pak)—all the snow that has fallen and stayed on a slope

# READ MORE

**O'Shei, Tim.** *Disaster in the Mountains!: Colby Coombs' Story of Survival.* True Tales of Survival. Mankato, Minn.: Capstone Press, 2007.

**Shone, Rob.** *Avalanches and Landslides.* Graphic Natural Disasters. New York: Rosen Pub. Group, 2007.

**Spilsbury, Louise, and Richard Spilsbury.** *Landslides and Avalanches in Action.* Natural Disasters in Action. New York: Rosen Pub. Group, 2009.

# INTERNET SITES

FactHound offers a safe, fun way to find Internet sites related to this book. All of the sites on FactHound have been researched by our staff.

Here's all you do:

Visit *www.facthound.com*

Type in this code: 9781429684170

Check out projects, games and lots more at
**www.capstonekids.com**

# INDEX